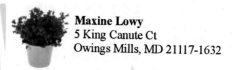
Maxine Lowy
5 King Canute Ct
Owings Mills, MD 21117-1632

D1174307

"THERE ONCE WAS A MAN FROM CANAAN..." **THE FIVE BOOKS** OF **LIMERICK**

Published in Israel by Joe Black
Book and jacket design by Eddie Goldfine
Printed by Ilan Press Ltd., Ashdod, Israel

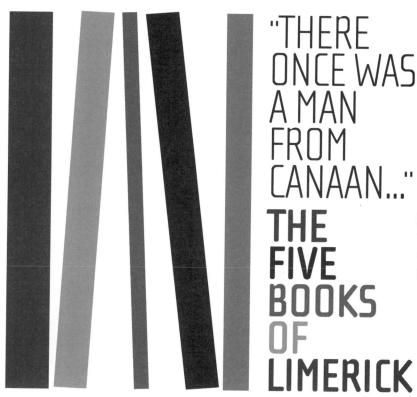

Rabbi Joe Black

"THERE ONCE WAS A MAN FROM CANAAN..."
THE FIVE BOOKS OF LIMERICK

This book would not have been possible without the encouragement of congregants, friends and fans of my music and writing. Thank you all for your support and love.

To Sue, Elana and Ethan: Thank you for tolerating my attempts at humor and even laughing every now and then.

To my best friend and brother from another mother, Eddie Goldfine: Thanks for your creativity and encouragement.

To all of my colleagues and the leadership of Temple Emanuel, Denver: Thank you for allowing me to share my love of Torah with you.

Special thanks to Susie Sigman and Sue Black for proofing and editing.

To all of the people who donated to our Kickstarter campaign – we could not have done this without you.

I especially want to recognize Rabbi Lisa Tzur, Sophie Black, Nancy Weinberger, Jon and Judie Harris, Reva Rosenbloom, Amos Rosenbloom and Marsha McDonald and everyone else who has helped bring this project to reality.

A special note: This book is also dedicated to the memory of Larry Kaufman (z"l). Larry was a huge inspiration to me. When I first began posting my limericks online, he would always write his own limericks in response. He challenged me to become a better writer. May his memory be for a blessing.

CONTENTS:

INTRODUCTION

LIMERICK

Syllabification: lim·er·ick

Pronunciation: /ˈlim(ə)rik

A humorous, frequently bawdy, verse of three long and two short lines rhyming aabba, popularized by Edward Lear. (Oxford English Dictionary.)

As a songwriter and musician, I've always found limericks to be a wonderful blend of storytelling, rhythm and rhyme. As a rabbi, the challenge of finding five perfect lines of poetry to encapsulate every portion in the yearly cycle of Torah readings became something of an obsession for me as I approached my 25th year on the pulpit. I started sharing them with friends and posting them on social media. Soon, other people began posting their limericks in response. After receiving several requests to publish them in book form, I finally gave in.

My goal in writing this book is to teach, entertain, and inspire others to understand that Torah study can and should be multi-dimensional. Some of these limericks simply tell a story. Others refer to midrashic and Talmudic passages. Some portions have only one limerick – others have two or three. All of them are written with love. I hope you enjoy them and will share them in classes, sermons, around the Shabbat and seder table and anywhere that words of Torah are expressed.

From Canaan, there once was a man
Who was given a sanctified plan
That was idealistic
And monotheistic
And now I'm a part of his clan

Happy limericking!

~Joe

GENESIS : BERESHIT : בראשית

THE FOUNDATION STORIES OF HUMANITY LEADING UP TO THE ORIGINS OF THE CHILDREN OF ISRAEL.

We Meet Abraham and Sarah, Isaac and Rebekah, Jacob, Rachel and Leah. The Twelve Tribes are created. Names are changed, fratricide (almost) takes place. There is jealousy and tenderness; deception and destiny. The future of the Israelites is forged on the back of a slave-turned-ruler named Joseph. Our narrative shifts from wandering in and around Canaan to the land of Egypt where Joseph's fame provides a safe place for settlement. Jacob/Israel blesses his children before he dies.

BERESHIT בראשית
{GENESIS 1:1-6:8}

Preceding the act of Creation
There was darkness and desolation
The Divine Spirit hovered
Over depths that were covered
By the promise of new population

*

"Just take a bite," said the snake.
"Who cares if a rule you might break?
The fruit that you'll eat
Is so juicy and sweet
Think of the pies you could bake!"

NOACH נח
{GENESIS 6:9-11:32}

Whether by chance or design
Noah, by God was assigned
To save all Creation
Through utilization
Of his gopher wood custom cruise line

*

Noah, uncouth and quite gruff
Went out of the ark in a huff
But when Shem, Ham and Yafet
Saw him drunk in the buff, it
Truly was more than enough

*

In building their tower to the sky
The "Babelites" learned on the fly
That they can't be immortal, and
Their heavenly portal
Caused language to multiply

LECH-LECHA לֶךְ לְךָ
{GENESIS 12:1–17:27}

God said "Abram, leave all that you know
To an unknown place you shall go
I will bless those who bless you
Curse those who oppress you
Through your offspring shall my presence flow."

VAYERA וירא
{GENESIS 18:1-22:24}

To Abraham, God did request
"Kill Isaac, the one you love best"
As he raised up his knife
To take his son's life
God said, "Stop! It was only a test!"

CHAYEI SARAH חיי שרה
{GENESIS 23:1-25:18}

After Sarah dies and is buried
Isaac, then must be married
Rivka brings relief
For poor Isaac's grief
When into his tent she is carried

תולדות TOLDOT
{GENESIS 25:19–28:9}

While Jacob was cooking a meal
Esau returned from the field
He said "Gimme some stew!"
Jake said, "Sure, just eschew
Your birthright and all of its yield."

VAYETZE ויצא
{GENESIS 28:10-32:3}

Fleeing Esau, Jacob must go
To Haran where his fortune would grow
He dreamed- angels ascended
And then comprehended
God was here - and I didn't know!

VAYISHLACH וישלח
{GENESIS 32:4-36:43}

Jacob bids Laban farewell
And moves on to where Esau dwells
A strange man he does fight
'Til the morning's sunlight
And receives a new name, Yisrael

VAYESHEV וישב
{GENESIS 37:1-40:23}

Joseph, the favorite son
Through his dreams has annoyed everyone
His brothers they pitch
Him into a ditch
And that's how our story's begun

MIKETZ מקץ
{GENESIS 41:1–44:17}

Pharaoh dreams of cows and of wheat
Fat, lean, sickly and sweet
His advisors all fail
But Joseph, in jail
Interprets - he's back on his feet

VAYIGASH ויגש
{GENESIS 44:18–47:27}

To his brothers, Joseph said, "I've...
Decided no more to connive.
You thought me deceased,
Now my fortune's increased
I am Joseph! Is Jacob alive?"

VAYECHI ויחי
{GENESIS 47:28–50:26}

With Menasheh and Ephraim
Israel takes his sweet time
While on his death bed
He crosses hands o'er their head
And pronounces the blessing sublime

EXODUS : SHEMOT : שמות

A NEW PHARAOH ARRIVES ON THE SCENE WHO "KNEW NOT JOSEPH." THE ISRAELITES ARE ENSLAVED – THEIR LIVES EMBITTERED BY HARD WORK.

We meet Moses - the son of a Levite who grew up in Pharaoh's palace. Moses sees the plight of his people and becomes a fighter for freedom. He flees from Pharaoh's wrath into the wilderness where he encounters the Divine presence in a burning bush. God instructs Moses to return to Egypt and lead his people through the wilderness into the Promised Land. ten plagues and a split sea later, the Children of Israel begin their forty year journey. They receive the Ten Commandments, build a golden calf and a tabernacle.

SHEMOT שמות
{EXODUS 1:1-6:1}

A new Pharaoh sat on the throne
But Joseph to him was not known
Of the Jews he said rudely
"We must deal with them shrewdly
Lest they try to make Egypt their own."

VA'ERA וארא
{EXODUS 6:2-9:35}

Moses shows what God will unveil
To Pharaoh with great detail
The Nile River, muddy
Will turn gross and bloody
Then come frogs, lice, flies, mange, boils, and hail

בא BO
{EXODUS 10:1–13:16}

The last of the plagues is the worst
The death of the children born first
Pharaoh's heart it is broken
God's decree has been spoken
four centuries of slavery's reversed

BESHALLACH בשלח
{EXODUS 13:17-17:16}

The Israelites crossing the sea
Comprehend that at last they are free
When the waters they part
They sing from their heart
"O God who is like unto Thee?"

יתרו YITRO
{EXODUS 18:1–20:23}

At Sinai the shofar was sounded
While thunder and lightning abounded
We stood side by side
While Moses inscribed
Ten laws on which our faith is founded

MISHPATIM משפטים
{EXODUS 21:1-24:18}

Though some may think fighting uncouth
Close reading reveals the truth
If damage ensues
Then payment is due
In cash, not eye, limb or tooth

TERUMAH תרומה
{EXODUS 25:1-27:19}

Moses gave an elaborate list
For the Mishkan that did consist
Of lapis lazuli
Gold, silver and jewelry
So God could live in our midst

TETZAVEH תצווה
{EXODUS 27:20–30:10}

The High Priest has fabulous clothes
Resplendent from head to his toes
With his urim and thummim
And colors a bloomin'
People see him wherever he goes

כי תיסע KI TISSA
{EXODUS 30:11–34:35}

With Aaron in charge of the fold
The people could not be controlled
When they cried out for Moses
He took rings from their noses
And made them a calf of pure gold

ויקהל-פקודי VAYAKHEL/PEKUDEI
{EXODUS 35:1-40:38}

When the Mishkan was finally erected
The Israelites all felt connected
The people's largesse
Gave God an address
And the tablets were safely protected

LEVITICUS : VAYIKRA : ויקרא

PRIESTS ARE GIVEN THEIR UNIFORMS AND JOB DESCRIPTIONS.

We learn about morality, dietary laws, how to treat diseases of the skin and sexual afflictions. There are lots of sacrifices and celebrations. Purity is really important. So is holiness.

VAYIKRA ויקרא
{LEVITICUS 1:1–5:26}

The Olah is completely consumed
The Minchah is very perfumed
Zevach Shelamim
Sacrifice of well being
But with Asham and Chatat sin's presumed

TZAV צַו
{LEVITICUS 6:1–8:36}

Aaron and sons are ordained
Their job is carefully explained
It's oily and bloody
Messy and muddy
No wonder their robes get all stained!

שמיני SHEMINI
{LEVITICUS 9:1–11:47}

When offering up sacrifice
One must be very precise
Aaron's sons offered fire
That wasn't desired
And thus paid the ultimate price

TAZRIA תזריע
{LEVITICUS 12:1–13:59}

METZORA מצורע
{LEVITICUS 14:1–15:33}

If your skin is scaly and sore
And is oozing with grossness and gore
You'll be labeled "unclean"
'Til the priest intervenes
And dunks you in water that's pure

*

When studying parshat Metzora
You learn to never ignore... a
peculiar emission
Or painful condition
That's explained in detail in the Torah

ACHAREI MOT אחרי מות
{LEVITICUS 16:1–18:30}

On Yom Kippur each year without fail
You must take two pure goats that are male
The High Priest casts the dice
And one goat's sacrificed
While the other's sent to Azazeyl

KEDOSHIM קדושים
{LEVITICUS 19:1–20:27}

Kedoshim means "sacred" it's true
It's incumbent upon every Jew
To act with compassion
Good deeds not to ration
We're holy, 'cause God's holy too

EMOR אמור
{LEVITICUS 21:1–24:23}

When bringing a sacrifice
It's important to heed this advice
Levitical law
Says it can have no flaw
So check once and then check it twice

BEHAR בהר
{LEVITICUS 25:1–26:2}

BECHUKOTAI בחוקותי
{LEVITICUS 26:3–27:34}

If a parcel of land you obtain
And reap profit from grapevine or grain
Though you've plowed and you've sown it
You really don't own it
God gives and can take back again.

*

If you follow God's command
You will profit from tilling your land
But if you fail to obey
Such curses, oy vey!
It's quite simple. Do you understand?

NUMBERS : BAMIDBAR : במדבר

THE ISRAELITES ARE GETTING RESTLESS. A CENSUS IS TAKEN. SPIES ARE SENT OUT TO SCOUT OUT THE LAND.

Only Joshua and Caleb return with a positive report. God decides that an entire generation must die before entering into the Promised Land. There is rebellion after rebellion. Bilaam is hired to curse the Israelites. He blesses them instead. Moses' frustration with his people leads to the creation of a leadership council. It also causes him to disobey God by striking instead of speaking to a rock to get water. God punishes Moses by not allowing him to enter into Canaan with his people. Miriam and Aaron - Moses' siblings - die in the wilderness.

BAMIDBAR במדבר
{NUMBERS 1:1–4:20}

As Moses prepared to alight
On his journey through wilderness bright
He counted all of the men
Again and again
To see who'd be able to fight

NASO נשא
{NUMBERS 4:21–7:89}

If you suspect that your wife is untrue
Our text tells us what you must do
Drinking bitters will tell
If her stomach does swell
Then she's not only sleeping with you

*

If a Nazarite you want to be
You must follow these special rules three
Your hair can't be trimmed
Don't drink wine - it's a sin
And from corpses you always must flee

*

May God bless and guard your sacred space
May God's light fill your being with grace
May you always be true
So God's presence shines through
And reflects the true peace of God's face

BEHA'ALOTECHA בהעלתך
{NUMBERS 8:1-12:16}

With only the manna to eat
The Israelites wanted some meat
They cried and they wailed
'Til God sent some quail
Which rotted away at their feet

SHLACH LECHA שלח לך
{NUMBERS 13:1–15:41}

Moses sent spies out to scout
All chieftains beloved and devout
Of the 12 that he sent
Only 2 were content
To say, "We can take em', no doubt!"

KORACH קרח
{NUMBERS 16:1–18:32}

Korach attemped a coup
Which caused a big hullabaloo
But his plan it went south
With the earth's opened mouth
He was swallowed with all of his crew

CHUKAT חוקת
{NUMBERS 19:1–22:1}

When you have a pure heifer that's red
Its burnt ashes are carefully spread
To be used for a cure
If you're labeled impure
By stumbling on someone who's dead

BALAK בלק
{NUMBERS 22:2–25:9}

Balak, he tried to suppress
The power that Israel possessed
He hired Bilaam
To curse them and run
But instead of a curse they got blessed

PINCHAS פנחס
{NUMBERS 25:10-30:1}

Pinchas, he got his reward
For zealous use of the sword
He made everything right
For the Israelites
When Cozbi and Zimri got gored

MATTOT מטות
{NUMBERS 30:2-32:42}

Gad, Menasheh and Reuven,
Thought the Jordan's East Bank was a-groovin'
So they said they'd fight first
Bear the brunt of the worst
But their cattle and kids they weren't movin'

MASEI מסעי
{NUMBERS 33:1-36:13}

Zelophchad he had daughters five
Whose inheritance kept them alive
But to find a good man
They must look in their clan
If Menasheh was to survive

DEUTERONOMY : BAMIDBAR : במדבר

THE RECAP. MOSES DELIVERS FOUR LONG SERMONS.

He reminds them of all that has taken place during their wandering in the wilderness. The TenCommandments are repeated and the Shema is proclaimed. Blessings and curses are detailed at length. Finally, God calls Moses to look out over the land that he will never get to enter. Moses dies and his burial place is never revealed.

DEVARIM דברים
{DEUTERONOMY 1:1–3:22}

Moses knew his life soon would be ended
His record he thus defended
Through a drawn-out oration
To the Israelite nation
Reminding them what they transcended

VA'ETHCHANAN ואתחנן
{DEUTERONOMY 3:23-7:11}

Eve and morning we're taught to recite
How to love God with heart, soul and might
On two tablets inscribed
To all the twelve tribes
Ten Commandments to do what is right

EKEV עקב
{DEUTERONOMY 7:12–11:25}

When you've tasted the fruits of the land
It's important that you understand
Though you've plowed and you've tilled
And your stomach's been filled
It all really came from God's hand

ראה RE'EH
{DEUTERONOMY 11:26–16:17}

God gives a commandment this day
A blessing for those who obey
But if you choose to ignore
Bad things are in store
Curses for turning away

SHOFTIM שופטים

{DEUTERONOMY 16:18-21:9}

For jurists to be fair and true
There are things that they never should do
Don't be blinded by bribes
Or a poor person's cries
Justice, justice shall you pursue

KI TETZE כי תצא
{DEUTERONOMY 21:10–25:19}

If you have a rebellious child
Who won't listen, gets drunk and is wild
We're taught to disown him
So the elders can stone him
(But not once was a case like this filed)

*

If, when building a house you forget
To furnish a parapet
If some careless clown
Should climb and fall down
His bruises could put you in debt

כי תבוא KI TAVO
{DEUTERONOMY 26:1-29:8}

If your lineage is pure European
You still must perform this routine -
When you bring your first fruits
To the priests you salute
"Dad was a roving Aramean"

NITZAVIM נִצָבִים
{DEUTERONOMY 29:9-30:20}

Together we all stood outside
A community unified
At the foot of the mount
We were called to account
To choose life with our arms open wide

VAYELEKH וילך
{DEUTERONOMY 31:1–31:30}

It was time for Moses to die
But before his final goodbye
He sang Joshua this song:
"Be courageous and strong
And on God you should always rely."

HA'AZINU האזינו
{DEUTERONOMY 32:1-32:52}

Moses' final oration
Was filled with recrimination
He told us "give ear"
So that we all would hear
How to shun future assimilation

VEZOT HA'BRACHA וזאת הברכה

{DEUTERONOMY 33:1–34:12}

Moses got a Divine embrace
Then God gave him his burial place
And all through the ages
There were no other sages
Who spoke up to God face to face

INDEX

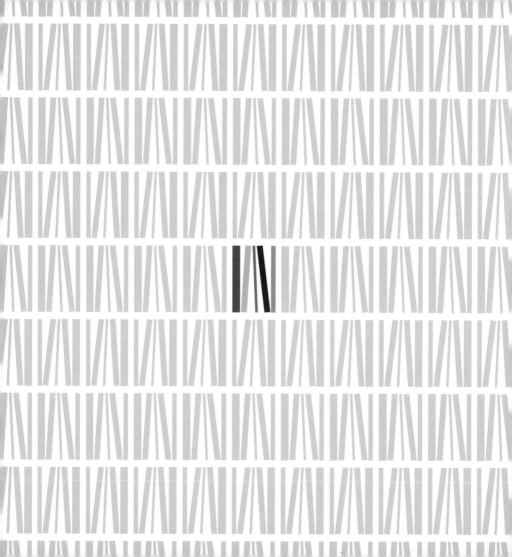